ILLUSTRATED ENCYCLOPEDIA
COMMUNICATION

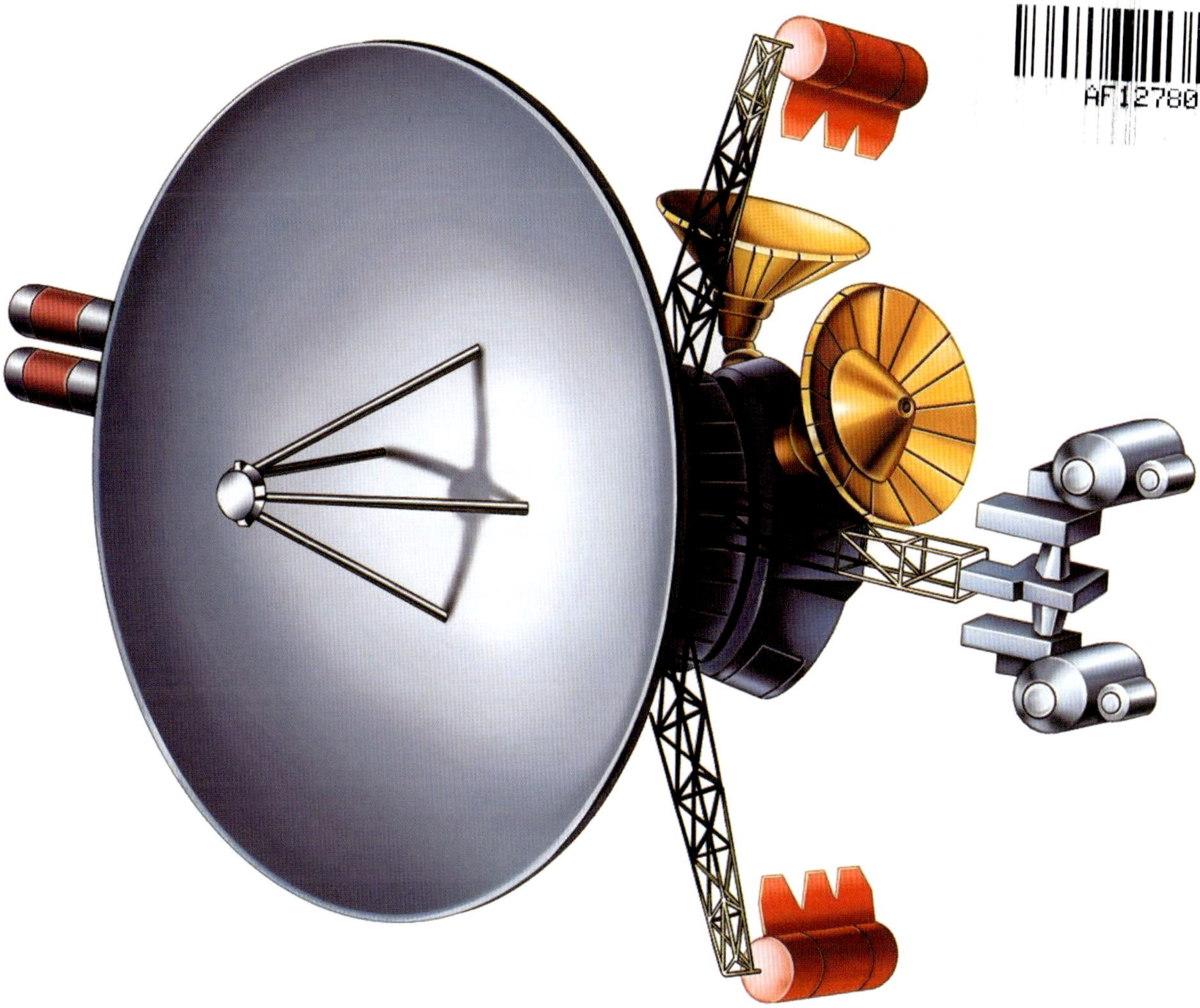

Managing Editor: Dr. Geeta Rani Arora
Editor: Ms. Pawanpreet Kaur
Education Consultant: Dr. Bimla Arora, *Shemrock School*
Copyright © with the publisher

Pegasus
An imprint of
B. Jain Publishers (P) Ltd.
USA - EUROPE - INDIA

COMMUNICATION

What is language?

Language is a vital means of communication. We use language, in form of sounds and conventional symbols, to express our thoughts and ideas to other people. Language is the mark of one's social and cultural identity. Language is important for our survival in society.

Oral Language

Oral language is the language that we speak and listen. We make use of sound, words, dialects, jargons, pitch and tone while speaking the language. Social communities assign different meanings to specific words. Human beings alter the shape of their mouth and vocal tract to produce a range of coherent sounds and utterances. More than 3,000 languages are spoken in the world today.

Non-verbal Language

Sometimes, we express our thoughts to other people without using the spoken word. We use gestures, body language, facial expressions, symbols and sign language to communicate without speaking.

Language helps us connect with people and it forges friendships, cultural ties and economic relationships.

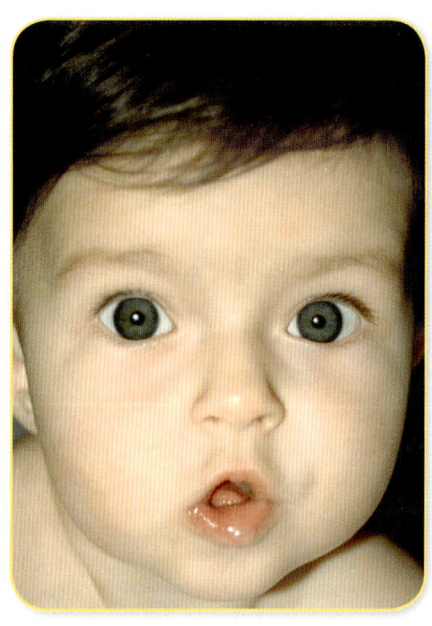

Non-verbal language— Facial expression showing surprise

Official applications, legal documents, newspaper editorials and crime reports are formal writings.

Written Language

A written language is the representation of a language by means of a writing system. Every social community has a specific type of writing style with different types of alphabets, letters, scripts and symbols. Written language can be preserved for a long time. Personal diaries, greeting cards and letters to friends are examples of informal writings.

LANGUAGE

Development of Language

No one knows how language began. Scholars believe that language developed very slowly from sounds like grunts, barks and hoots made by prehuman creatures. First a simple system of vocal communication evolved that became more complex with time. Writing appeared about 1,000 years after the origin of the spoken language. The earliest known written records are Sumerian word-pictures made around 3500 BC.

An early script on a clay tablet.

Linguistics

Linguistics is the scientific study of language. Scholars who study language are called linguists. Linguists explain how language is represented in the mind. They work on the internal structure of a language and try to find out the common elements of all languages. Noam Chomsky, an American linguist, is known as the father of modern linguistics.

Quick Look

Braille is a system of language that allows blind people to read by touch.

Language Cultures

Pidgin

Pidgin is a simplified language that develops when speakers from different linguistic backgrounds come in contact in situations such as trade, and slavery. Pidgins are not the native language of any community, but are learned as second languages. Usually a pidgin language is a rough blend of the vocabulary of one cultural group (often dominant) with the structure of the other (often dependent) group.

Most people around the world speak English in different forms.

Creole

Creole is a language that was originally a pidgin but has become nativised, that is, a community of speakers claims it as their first language. Majority of creole languages are based on English, Portuguese, French and Spanish that are blended with local languages. Examples of creole are the Gullah of South Carolina and Georgia (based on English), and the creole of Haiti (based on French).

Dialect

A dialect is a regional variety of a main language. A dialect differs in its vocabulary, speech patterns and pronunciation from other regional varieties of the same main language. For example, Spanish has many different dialects.

COMMUNICATION

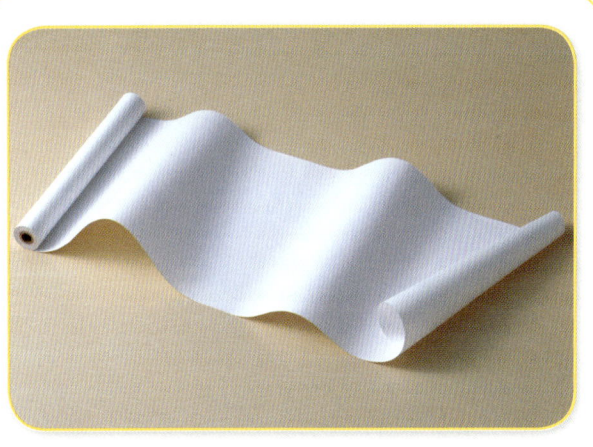

Many printed papers are bound together to hinge at one edge to make a book.

Different qualities of paper are used for different kind of uses.

What is paper?

Paper is a thin sheet material made of fibers used for writing and printing. The word 'paper' was derived from the word 'papyrus', a plant grown abundantly in Egypt. In ancient times, Egyptians, Greeks and Romans used this plant for making their writing material called papyrus. Today, paper is made from pulps of cellulose fibers, such as wood, cotton or flax.

Papermaking

The method of papermaking was invented by Chinese in 105 AD. Ts'ai Lun, an official from the court of emperor Ho-Ti of Han Dynasty, was the first to invent the papermaking method. Ts'ai Lun made paper from a mixture of finely chopped mulberry, hemp rags and water. He mashed the mixture flat, pressed the water out and dried it in the sun. Ts'ai Lun's paper was used all over the China very soon.

Johannes Gutenberg

Johannes Gutenberg is known for his invention of the printing press in 1440. He was a German craftsman and inventor. His movable type printing machine used metal moulds, alloys, oil-based inks, and a special press. Gutenberg's printing press made possible the mass production of printed books. Gutenberg also taught printing to many people.

Johannes Gutenberg

Paper and Printing

Paper Uses

Industry	Uses
Agriculture	Sacks, seed packets.
Building	Wallpaper, roofing, flooring, decorative laminates for furniture.
Communication	Writing, typing, printing, envelopes, publishing, accounts, receipts, stamps, newspapers, magazines, greeting cards, calendars, diaries, telephone directories.
Office Paper	Photocopying paper, graph papers, paper twine and string, blotting paper, carbonless paper, box files, folders.
Education	Books, exercise books, instruction books, maps, wall-charts, report cards.
Business	Computer tapes, print-out sheets, advertisements, circulars, catalogues, filing systems, sales and service manuals, brochures, shop-till paper.
Domestic Products	Wrapping and boxes for cleaning materials, domestic tissues, paper plates and cups, kitchen towels, table napkins, lamp shades.
Food Packaging	Wrapping for bread, flour, tea, sugar, butter, margarine, sweets, deep frozen food, etc., milk cartons, egg boxes, foil wrappings, tea bags, sausage skins.
Entertainment and Sport	Menu cards, paper hats, crackers, fireworks, program playing cards, board games, kites, model aircraft, football coupons, race cards.

Quick Look

The first printed newspaper was seen in China in 740 AD after the invention of woodblock printing in 600 AD.

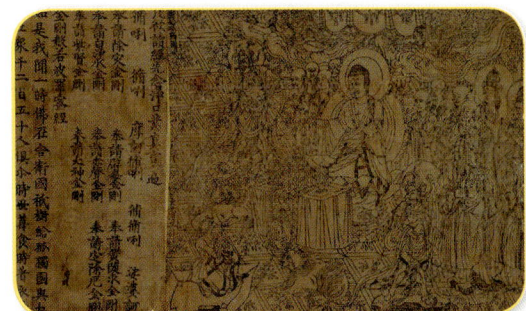

Diamond Sutra

Printing Milestones

Date	Milestone
888	The Diamond Sutra, a Buddhist scripture, was the first dated example of block printing.
1041	Bi Sheng in China invented movable clay type.
1423	Use of xylography to produce books started by Europeans.
1436	Gutenberg begins work on his printing press.
1440	Invention of Gutenberg's wooden press, which used movable metal type.
1444	Gutenberg sets up a printing shop.
1452	Gutenberg begins printing the 42-line Bible in two volumes.
1455	First block-printed Bible, the Biblia Pauperum, published in Germany.
1461	The first illustrated book 'Edelstein' was printed by Albrecht Pfister.
1499	Printing had become established in more than 2,500 cities around Europe.
1499	An estimated 15 million books have been press printed.

COMMUNICATION

Post Office

The Post office is a facility where postal services are available. Post offices form a network of office branches where mails and letters are collected, sorted and sent to their destination. The Post offices are located in every town and village, and deliver letters even to remote areas. The Post box is a later development of the post office, where one can drop postcards or letters.

Postal Codes

Postal codes are a combination of 6 digits meant as postal address codes. Postal codes aid in the sorting of mail. Postal codes were first experimented in Norwich, UK in October 1959. UK postal codes are known as postcodes and are alphanumeric. Every country has its own design and placement rules for postal codes.

Postman

A postman is a person who delivers mails to homes and offices. The Postman is sometimes called "mailman," "mail carrier" or "letter carrier" in North America. In Australia, a postman is called "postie".

A postage stamp is an adhesive paper evidence of a fee paid for postal services.

The postman is an employee of the post office or postal service who delivers the post.

Each Pony Express rider rode about 121 kilometers per day.

Pony Express

The Pony Express was an early American mail service. Horse riders carried mails between St. Joseph, Missouri, and San Francisco, California, covering a distance of 3,164 kilometers. The Pony Express ran day and night, summer and winter between 157 relay stations, located 8 to 32 kilometers apart.

Postal Service

United States Postal Service

Item	1980	1990	1995	1996	1997	1998	1999
Offices, stations, and branches	39,486	40,067	39,149	38,212	38,019	38,159	38,169
Number of post offices	30,326	28,959	28,392	28,189	28,060	27,952	27,893
Number of stations and branches	9,160	11,108	10,757	10,023	9,959	10,207	10,276
Pieces of mail handled (mil.)	106,311	166,301	180,734	183,440	190,888	196,905	201,576
Employees, total (1,000)	667	843	875	886	893	905	906

Airmail

Airmail is the carriage of mail by air. The first regular airmail service began in 1870 from Paris by balloon. Airmail stamps usually have wings, an airplane, or some other symbol of flying on them. The first airmail stamp was issued by Italy in 1917.

'Stamp collecting' is the extremely popular hobby of collecting postage stamps.

Post offices sort mails by postal codes.

Quick Look

The first transpacific airmail was sent in 1935, while the first transatlantic airmail was sent in 1939.

Postal Service Milestones

1516
King Henry VIII established the office of "Master of the Posts."

1635
Charles I made the Royal Mail service available to the public for the first time with postage being paid by the recipient.

1847
The United States issues its first stamps.

1849
France issues its first stamps.

1849
Belgium issues its first stamps.

1852
The United States issues its first stamped envelopes.

1855
The United States issues Registered Mail.

1855
Compulsory prepayment of postage in the United States.

1858
Street letter boxes in the United States.

1887
International parcel post.

1893
First commemorative stamps in the United States.

1911
United States creates a postal savings system.

COMMUNICATION

What is a newspaper?

The Newspaper is a publication of news and articles on folded sheets of cheap, low-quality paper called newsprint. A Newspaper contains news, opinions, articles and advertisements. Newspapers are usually published daily or weekly.

Daily Newspaper

The Daily newspapers are published everyday. They cover local events, national events and world events. Daily newspapers also carry editorials, feature articles, and news about entertainment and sports. The production of a daily newspaper is a complex process that involves great speed and efficiency from correspondents, reporters, photographers and other staff members.

Weekly Newspaper

Weekly newspapers are published once or twice a week. They are smaller than daily newspapers and are more popular in small communities or territories. Some weekly newspapers mainly cover news on business and sports.

Trajan's Forum in Rome

Newspapers are published in all major languages of the world.

USA Today, Wall Street Journal, New York Times, Times London and The Guardian are famous newspapers.

Acta Diurna

The *Acta Diurna* or "Daily Acts/Gazette" is considered a prototype of the modern newspaper. The *acta* were official notices that the Roman government published almost 2,000 years ago. The *acta* were posted daily in a public place, like the Forum and contained official and general information for the Roman public.

NEWSPAPERS

World Newspaper Circulation

Country	Circulation
China	93.5 million a day
India	78.8 million a day
Japan	70.4 million a day
United States	48.3 million a day
Germany	22.1 million a day

Broadsheet newspaper

Newspaper Sizes

Newspapers are published in two major formats—standard and tabloid. Standard-sized newspapers are larger and usually have eight columns. Tabloids are printed in a smaller format and are generally half the size of a broadsheet newspaper.

Times of India

The *Times of India* is the largest selling English broadsheet newspaper in the world. Around 2.4 million copies of *The Times of India* are sold every day.

Quick Look

The world's oldest newspaper is *Post-och Inrikes Tidningar*. It was first published in Sweden in 1645.

Newspaper Milestones

59 BC
Acta Diurna, the first newspaper, is published in Rome.

1556
Notizie Scritte, the first monthly newspaper, is published in Venice.

1605
'Relation', the first printed newspaper, is published weekly in Antwerp.

1690
Publick Occurrences, America's first newspaper, is published.

1702
Daily Courant, the first English language daily newspaper, is published.

1704
Daniel Defoe, the world's first journalist, publishes the *Review*.

1803
The Sydney Gazette and *New South Wales Advertiser* are the first newspapers to be published in Australia.

1856
The first full-page newspaper ad is published in the *New York Ledger*.

1871
Yokohama Mainichi Shimbun, the first daily newspaper, is published in Japan.

1885
Newspapers are delivered daily by train.

1903
The first tabloid style newspaper, the *Daily Mirror,* is published.

COMMUNICATION

What is a book?

A book is a collection of written, printed, or illustrated work or composition that has been published. A single sheet within a book is called a leaf, and each side of a leaf is called a page.

Harry Potter

Harry Potter is one of the most popular books series worldwide. J. K. Rowling, the author of the book, is the first person to earn more than $1 billion from writing. Translated in about 63 languages, over 300 million copies of the whole series of Harry Potter have been sold.

E-books

E-books or electronic books are modern books that can be downloaded from Internet. Electronic books are in use since 20 years. Early e-books could not store much information and were difficult to read. Modern e-books are small, and light to hold and contain large volumes of information.

Books are a storehouse of knowledge and information.

A book where we find a collection of words with similar meanings is known as a Thesaurus.

Types of Books

Atlas – a book containing maps of continents, countries with the political boundaries and physical features.
Dictionary – a book with an alphabetical list of words and their meanings.
Encyclopedia – a book with an alphabetical list of topics and subjects with an extensive description.
Fairy tale – a story book for children that are retold again and again, and contain fairies and imaginative characters.
Novel – a fictional book of a long story.
Yearbook – a chronological collection of events and their description of the previous year.

Books and Libraries

Book Facts

Book Name	Description
Bhutan: A Visual Odyssey Across The Kingdom	This collection of photographs is the largest book ever published. It measures 2.1 X 1.5 cm.
The World's Smallest Book	Published by Joshua Richert and measures 2.4 X 2.9 cm
La Compagne des Glaces	Longest novel written by Georges-Jean Arnaud
The Diary of Anne Frank	Translated into more than 55 languages
The Birds of America	The most expensive printed book sold for $8,000,000

Library

A library is a collection of books on different subjects. Libraries also include other printed materials like manuscripts, periodicals, maps, photographs, journals, etc. Some countries have mobile libraries. In Kenya, camels carry books and mobile tents. Boats and bikes are also used as mobile libraries.

Quick Look
Bible has been the world's all time best selling book with about 2.5 to 6 billion sold copies.

Readers locate books in a library by referring catalogues.

Famous Libraries

British Library
The British Library in London, UK was founded in 1753. It consists of collections of physicians and earls and many private collections. It has a collection of 18,000,000 books.

Library of Congress
The U.S. Library of Congress in Washington, D.C. USA, was founded in 1800. It has a collection of about 29,000,000 books.

Harvard University Library
Harvard University Library in Cambridge, Massachusetts, USA, was founded in 1990. It has a collection of 11,300,000 books.

COMMUNICATION

Radio

Radio is a communication device that transmits messages using radio-waves. It is one of the most important and popular modes of communication today. Most communication devices use radio-waves to transmit words, music, codes and other signals to different parts of the world. Radio broadcasts music, news, discussions, interviews, advertisements, cultural and sports events.

Radio waves can transmit sound, video and data through the air.

Guglielmo Marconi

Guglielmo Marconi was an Italian electrical engineer who invented the radio. He became the first person to successfully transmit radio signals across a distance of 1.6 kilometers in 1895. After some years, he used his radio device to send signals across the Atlantic Ocean. Marconi received the Nobel Prize in 1909 for his important contribution in developing radio communication.

Guglielmo Marconi invented radio.

Radio Station

A radio station is a place where music, news and other broadcasts are produced and transmitted. The radio programs that have to be transmitted are either in the recorded form or are performed live. Each radio station is assigned with its own frequency. Listeners tune into that particular frequency by adjusting the frequency dials of their radio sets.

Every radio station creates its own programs and transmitting schedules.

Quick Look

In 1878, the first telephone exchange was opened in New Haven, Connecticut, USA.

RADIO

AM

AM stands for Amplitude Modulation. It is a technique used for transmitting information through radio waves. In this technique, the amplitude of transmitting radio waves is changed according to the changes in audio-frequency waves. It is the most popular form of radio transmission. It is still widely used all over the world.

FM

FM stands for Frequency Modulation. It is a technique in which the frequency of carrier waves is changed according to the changes in the audio-frequency waves. Frequency Modulation is used to provide high quality sound over broadcast radio. Edwin Howard Armstrong, an American electrical engineer and inventor, developed FM radio broadcasting.

Ham Radio

The Ham radio is a system of communication in which people use various types of radio equipments to communicate with other individuals with similar radio equipments. People who communicate using ham radio are known as 'hams'. People use ham radios for public service and recreation.

Digital Audio Broadcasting

Digital Audio Broadcasting (DAB) started in UK in 1995. DAB gives better quality reception and easy tuning to listeners. In 2002, BBC launched five DAB channels and within 2 years 1 million DAB digital radios had been sold.

The first commercial radio services began on AM.

Edwin Howard Armstrong

People also use ham radios for self-training.

13

COMMUNICATION

What is a television?

The Television is one of the most important means of communication and entertainment. It is a device that transmits electronic presentation of pictures and sounds. Television let millions of people in the world to connect with the rest of the world via news, entertainment, sports, information and commercials.

John Logie Baird

Many people contributed to the invention of the television over the years. John Logie Baird invented the first mechanical television system. In 1920, Baird used transparent rods to transmit images to television and created the first televised pictures of objects in motion in 1924. The first simultaneous sound and vision telecast was broadcast in 1930.

A newsroom is the place where reporters, editors, technicians work together to broadcast news on television.

John Logie Baird invented the world's first working television system.

Quick Look

In 1936, the United Kingdom was the first country to have television. USA, USSR, France and Brazil followed over the next few years.

Countries with maximum number of TV sets

Country	TVs Per 1,000 People in 2006	Country	TVs Per 1,000 People in 2006
Norway	1,552	Latvia	859
Bermuda	1,070	Japan	843
UK	1,101	Netherlands	761
Denmark	975	Australia	724
Romania	893	Canada	706
USA	882	Ireland	694

TELEVISION

Number of Television Broadcast Stations

Country	Number of Stations	Date of Formation
Russia	7,306	1998
China	3,240	1997
European Union	2,700	1995
United States	2,218	2006
United Kingdom	729	2001
Ukraine	647	2006
France	584	1995
India	562	1997
South Africa	556	1997
Germany	373	1995
Italy	358	1995
Japan	211	1999
Australia	104	1997

Plasma TV

Plasma televisions are flat panel televisions ranging from 42 to 102 inches. They produce images by xenon and neon gas, which are located between two panels of glass. Plasma televisions are becoming more and more popular today in households. The clear picture quality and the screen size are the main advantages of plasma televisions.

Laser TV

Laser televisions are advanced technology, thin-screened televisions. They use the power of laser to display sharp and well toned images on screen. A Laser TV displays about 80% of the colours visible to the human eye. It displays richer and more vibrant colour patterns than the conventional plasma or LCD displays. Laser TVs last long and require less power.

Watching television is a form of entertainment.

Television programs are made in a television studio like the one shown in the picture.

COMMUNICATION

Telephone

The Telephone is one of the most important means of communication. It allows people to talk to one another at a distance beyond the range of human voice. All telephone calls are routed through a telephone exchange.

The Name

The word 'telephone' is derived from two Greek words. *Tele* in Greek means "far" and *phone* means "sound."

Cordless Phone

Cordless telephones are portable, wireless telephones with a limited range of mobility. Cordless telephones communicate via radio waves and were introduced in the 1970s. Cordless phones are powered by battery, which needs to be recharged.

The First Telephone

Alexander Graham Bell invented the telephone in 1876. One day, while working on a telegraph machine, Bell heard it transmitting sounds. This incident led him to invent the telephone. Bell's telephone could transmit and receive human speech.

Dial Tone

Dial tone is a sound that a caller hears on the telephone handset. The sound signifies that the telephone is ready to make or receive a telephone call.

Telephone handsets have screens displaying call records.

The father of the cordless phone is George Sweigert, an American radio operator.

Alexander Graham Bell also invented phonograph.

Cellular Phones

A cellular phone is a wireless phone that operates on a cellular network. It is connected to a base station. Cellular phones play an important role in communication. Most modern mobile phone systems are cell-structured. Radio waves are used to communicate between a handset and nearby cell sites.

Digital Telephony

Digital telephony is a system of modern telephony, which has replaced old telephonic methods. Digital telephony transfers data at high speed over great distances, using optical fibers.

Quick Look

In 1878, the first telephone exchange was opened in New Haven, Connecticut, USA.

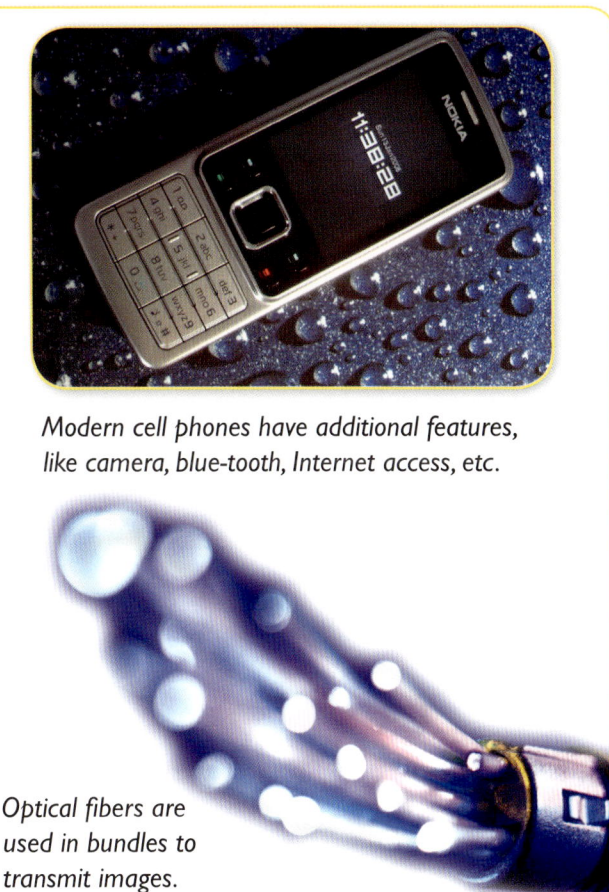

Modern cell phones have additional features, like camera, blue-tooth, Internet access, etc.

Optical fibers are used in bundles to transmit images.

Telephone Facts

June 2, 1875 Alexander Graham Bell transmits the sound of a plucked steel reed using electromagnet instruments.

March 7, 1876 Bell's US patent, 174,465, for the telephone is granted.

March 10, 1876 Bell transmits first telephone conversation "Mr. Watson, come here, I want to see you."

August 10, 1876 Alexander Bell makes world's first long distance telephone call between Paris, France and Brantford, Ontario, Canada.

February 4, 1878 Thomas Edison demonstrates telephone between Menlo Park, New York and Philadelphia, at a distance of 210 kilometers.

January 25, 1915 First transcontinental telephone call between Alexander Graham Bell and Thomas Watson.

1927 First public Transatlantic phone call (via radio).

May 28, 1927 Rotary dial service was started from mid night.

1935 First telephone call around the world.

1946 First commercial mobile phone call.

1981 The world's first fully-automatic mobile phone system NMT is started in Sweden and Norway.

1982 Caller ID patented by Carolyn Doughty, Bell Labs.

1991 The GSM mobile phone network is started in Finland.

1995 Caller ID implemented nationally in USA.

COMMUNICATION

Music and Songs

Music is one of the most popular sources of entertainment. Music and songs play an important part in expressing and defining cultures and traditions. Music is influenced by society, politics, religion, climate and even technology. People also express their joys, sorrows and devotion to God through music and songs.

Ballads

Ballads are songs that tell stories of historical accounts or fairy tales. It is sung in a standard pattern with rhyming words, repetitive lines and chorus. Folk ballads are traditional stories of a particular culture that are orally passed down through generations.

Rock Music

Rock music is one of the world's most popular forms of music. It originated in the United States in the early 1950s. Elvis Presley, Bob Dylan and Madonna have remained the most famous rock stars, while The Beatles, Rolling Stones, Pink Floyd are some of the world's most famous rock bands.

A singing performance on a stage needs lot of practice.

Rock music is played using electric guitar, drums and keyboards.

The birthday song is sung while the birthday child cuts the cake.

The Most Famous Song

Two American sisters Mildred J. Hill and Patty Smith Hill wrote the song 'good morning to you...' in 1893 to sing in the school assemblies. In 1924, the lyrics of this song changed to 'happy birthday to you...' and it became popular throughout the world. Since then this song is sung at every birthday party in every corner of the world.

Music and Songs

The Beatles

The Beatles was an English rock band that became famous during 1960's for its rock and roll music. The band members were John Lennon, Paul McCarthy, George Harrison and Ringo Starr. Beatles popularized rock music throughout the world. Their music influenced the social and cultural revolutions of the 1960s. 'Beatlemania' was the term generally used to describe the excitement generated by their music.

A Georgian folk-rock band performing on the stage.

People singing in chorus at a festival.

Quick Look

The Longhorn Band of the University of Texas has a large drum nicknamed 'Big Bertha.' It has a circumference of 7.6 meters.

Hall of Fame

Mozart

Mozart was an Austrian born German musician who is looked upon as a musical genius of all times. Mozart composed hundreds of beautiful and unique music works, which include over 20 operas and about 15 masses. He was famous for his piano and violin concerts. He also performed over 50 symphonies and 20 sonatas that made him extremely popular with music lovers of his generation.

Ludwig van Beethoven

Ludwig van Beethoven was a German pianist who is also one of the most respected and influential composers of all times. He made crucial contributions to the Western classical music. Beethoven composed music in various genres including symphonies, sonatas, masses and operas. His compositions for various orchestras grew hugely famous in his time. He also performed in piano and violin concerts.

COMMUNICATION

Cinema and its Role

Cinema is the art and business of making films, motion pictures or movies. Cinema has evolved as the most popular form of entertainment throughout the world. Apart from entertainment, cinema also plays an educative and informative role in society. It helps people to explore several social issues, like terrorism, crime, poverty, etc, and thus stimulates social changes.

Charlie Chaplin

Charlie Chaplin was a notable English comedian, filmmaker and musician. He created films in which he acted himself. He portrayed himself as a downtrodden little man in baggy pants and bowler hat. The little man moved around in a world full of chaos but remained positive in his outlook. He smiled even in a miserable situation making his audience cheerful.

Oscar Award

The Oscars are most prestigious of all film awards. They are presented by the Academy of Motion Picture Arts and Sciences to directors, actors and writers for their exellence in films.

A Japanese film poster of Akira Kurosawa's Seven Samurai.

Charlie Chaplin's films are popular throughout the world even now.

Steven Spielberg also won the best director Oscar for 'Saving Private.'

Steven Spielberg

Steven Spielberg is one of the most influential and commercially successful film directors in the history of Hollywood. 'Jaws', 'Jurassic Park' and 'Raiders of the Lost Ark' are some of the superhits directed by him. Spielberg received Oscars for his movie 'Schindler's List' in 1994.

CINEMA

Film Studio

A film studio is a place with controlled environment meant for making movies. Major film production companies have their own movie studios. The Hollywood studio system is dominated by six global entertainment companies: Time Warner, Viacom, Fox, Sony, NBC Universal and Disney. These companies also produce films for other filmmaking companies.

Gorky Film Studio, Russia.

James Cameron

James Cameron is one of the most innovative directors of the Hollywood. Also a producer and screenwriter, Cameron is noted for his action and science fiction films. 'The Terminator', 'Aliens', 'Terminator 2: Judgment Day', 'True Lies' are some of his films that made a big mark in the history of Hollywood. Cameron is majorly known for his blockbuster 'Titanic'.

Quick Look

Titanic broke box office records all over the world and swept the Academy Awards and 11 Oscars.

Stages of Cinema

Origin
The cinema originated during the late 19th century. In 1891, Thomas Edison displayed the first moving picture machine known as the Kinetoscope. Early movies were silent and lasted for about 20 minutes.

1920s
Films became bigger, costlier and more polished. America became the world's leading producer of films.

1930s
Sound, dialogues and colours were introduced to the cinema. Different genres, like romance, comedy, horror and gangster films, developed.

1940s
Films became a source of escape and relief from the World War traumas.

1950s
The cinema incorporated middle-class values. This decade also saw the rise of modern jazz and was one of the best decades for comedy films.

1960s
Cinema reflected the decade of fun, fashion, rock 'n' roll, and social issues like youth movements, women's liberation movement and transitional cultural values.

1970s
The counter-culture of the time influenced Hollywood to be freer, to take more risks and to experiment with alternative, young filmmakers.

1980s
The era was characterized by the introduction of 'high-concept' films. Film budgets skyrocketed due to special effects.

1990s
Multi-screen cineplex complexes introduced.

2000s
An era of remakes, adaptations, re-treads of classic TV shows or books and creation of sequels of recent blockbusters.

COMMUNICATION

What is a theatre?

A theatre is an art form to entertain people. Theatre artists, actors and performers give live performances before an audience. Theatre performances include circus, musical concerts, plays, comedy shows, talk shows, etc. They are performed in a theatre, an auditorium or in a specially built space.

Opera

The Opera is a form of theatre that is a combination of drama and music. The story of the drama is conveyed by songs rather than dialogues and scripts. The building designed for opera performances are called opera houses.

Play

A play is a theatre performance of a story or literary work written by a dramatist or a playwright. The actors act the characters of the story according to the screenplay. Plays can be comic, satirical, tragic, historical or romantic.

New York State Theatre at Lincoln center.

A theatre performance.

Orchestra is a form of musical concert.

Musical Concerts

Musical concerts are live performances by musicians before an audience. Musical concerts include performances by a single musician or by an orchestra, choir or a band. Large concerts that last for many days and involve performances by many musical groups are known as festivals. For example, Bloodstock Open Air is a heavy metal festival held annually at Catton Hall in England.

Theatre

Famous Theatres

Name	Built	Place	Description
The Golden Globe	Around 600 BC	London, UK	Famous theatre of Shakespeare. This large, roofless building was once about 11 meters high and 30 meters in diameter. Now it is only to 1.5 meters high and has a diameter of 15 meters.
New York State Theatre	1964-65	New York City, USA	Is part of New York City's Lincoln Centre for the Performing Arts complex. It is home to both New York City Ballet and New York City Opera.
Sydney Opera House	1959-73	Sydney, Australia	One of the most famous performing theatres in the world. It is situated on Bennelong Point in Sydney Harbor.

Quick Look

The word *theatre* is derived from a Greek word meaning "a place for seeing."

Sydney Opera House.

Theatre Buildings

Theatre buildings have three basic parts, auditorium, stage and behind-the-scene space.

Auditorium

A theatre auditorium is the area built for the audience to sit and watch the performance. It has well-managed facilities for audience like clear sound system, comfortable seating arrangement, food courts, toilets, etc.

Stage

Stage is the place in a theatre where performers perform the play or concert. Proscenium stage and open stage are two types of indoor stage. In proscenium stage, the acoustic space is different for both stage and auditorium. In open stage, both have the same acoustic space.

Behind-the-scene space

It includes the space for dressing rooms, make-up space, light and sound systems. It also has space to make costumes, scenery, and storage space for costumes, lighting instruments and scenery equipments.

Inside the auditorium.

COMMUNICATION

Advertising

Advertising is a system of communication whose purpose is to promote a product, service or an idea. Various companies, social organizations, political parties and government use advertisements to inform public about their products, services and agendas. Advertisements have an enormous influence on people's lives, as they encourage people to eat a certain type of food, wear certain types of clothes, use certain types of electronic goods, etc.

An advertisement promoting Maggi noodles.

Mobile Billboards

Mobile billboards are large publicity boards mounted on trucks or large vehicles. Mobile billboards are used for advertising on highways or crowded roads. These billboards display large advertisements to passing pedestrians and drivers. Mobile billboards usually have witty slogans, bright visual displays and spotlights that easily catch the attention of people coming from a distance.

Some mobile billboards display only one advertisement, while some rotate different advertisements.

Advertising agencies make advertisements for corporate companies to increase demand for their products and services.

Advertising Agency

Advertising agencies are organisations that are hired by companies to develop and manage advertisements and publicity campaigns on their behalf. Advertising agencies develop new ideas, catchy phrases and jingles to market and sell products. There are different types of advertising agencies. For example, tradigital agencies are advertising agencies that provide both traditional and digital advertising service.

ADVERTISING

Newspaper Advertisements

Newspapers are the medium through which large numbers of print advertisements reach the public every day. Newspapers make most of their money from advertising. Advertisers buy space in newspapers to publish their ads to promote products and services to readers. Newspapers carry two types of advertisements: display ads and classified ads.

Online Advertising

Advertising on the World Wide Web is a recent trend for delivering marketing messages and attracting customers. Examples of online advertising include contextual ads on search engine result pages (like Google), banner ads, pop-up windows, etc. These ads are believed to have a greater chance of attracting customers, because they share a similar context as the user's search query. For example, a search query on "flowers" brings advertisements of florist websites.

Television advertisements lure viewers with fascinating videos and jingles.

Television Advertisements

Television advertisements combine visual, audio and motion effects. Advertisers buy time slots on television for their ads. TV ads are intelligently inserted between television programs so that viewers cannot easily avoid them. All television ads are short and have snappy jingles, catchy punch lines and bright visuals.

Quick Look

Catchy words or phrases used in advertisements, which are a brand or a product recognisable, are known as punch lines.

World's Top 10 Advertising Agencies

1. AMV BBDO
2. McCann Erickson
3. M&C Saatchi
4. Bartle Bogle Hegarty
5. JWT London
6. WCRS
7. RKCR/Y&R
8. Euro RSCG London
9. Publicis
10. DDB London

COMMUNICATION

What is E-mail?

E-mail is an electronic message sent via the Internet or any telecommunications network. E-mails are typically composed and sent from computers or mobile phones. E-mails are usually in the form of a text, but graphic images, sound and video files can be sent as attachments.

First E-mail

In 1969, Professor Leonard Kleinrock of UCLA and a small group of his students sent the first electronic message to a Stanford University computer. Three years later, in late 1971, Ray Tomlinson sent the first network e-mail in history.

E-mail Address

Computer engineer, Ray Tomlinson began the use of @ sign in e-mail addresses. He used the @ symbol in his first E-mail. The sign is put between the user's login name and the name of the host computer.

Unlike postal mails, e-mails are delivered in a few minutes.

In 1993, America Online and Delphi connected their e-mail systems to the Internet. With this began the large-scale use of Internet e-mail.

Online Chat

Online chat is one-on-one or group communication over the Internet. Online chat is text-based. Chat tools usually include instant messengers, Internet Relay Chat, and talkers. Friendly conversations or official meetings also happen on video chat or webcam chat. Webcams are video capturing devices connected to computers.

Internet cafes provide Internet access for a fee.

Email and Internet Chat

Popular Chat Programs on the Internet

- AOL Instant Messenger (AIM)
- Windows Live Messenger
- Yahoo! Messenger
- QQ
- Skype
- AIM
- Internet Relay Chat (IRC)
- Jabber
- eBuddy
- ICQ
- Xfire
- PalTalk
- Camfrog
- Gadu-Gadu
- Google Talk
- Pichat
- Talk
- Talker

Instant Messaging

Instant messaging is a form of online communication. Instant messaging allows two or more people to send and receive text messages in real time. Instant messaging allows both private and community conversations over a network such as the Internet.

QQ

QQ is the most popular free instant messaging service in China. It is also the world's third most popular instant messaging service. QQ has over 340 million users, mostly from Mainland China.

Offline Messaging

Offline messaging allows users to send messages to contacts who are offline. Offline messages can be read by the recipient when he/she comes online.

Quick Look

Emoticons or smileys are online facial expressions and gestures.

Netiquette or Internet etiquette are rules of accepted and proper behaviour on the Internet.

Chat forums like Yahoo! Messenger, g-talk, Skype also have an application of voice chat.

COMMUNICATION

Online News

News that appears on the World Wide Web is known as online news. There are many online news channels, like BBC and Fox News that provide updated information about recent and important events happening in the world. The news is transported on the Internet using the Network News Transport Protocol or NNTP.

News Portal

News Portal is a news related website that provides links to useful news pages.

Blog

A blog is a website where entries are made by people in a journal style. People post their comments in an interactive format regarding various topics, including social, political, religious, literary or academic issues. A typical blog combines text, images, and links to other blogs, web pages, and other media related to its topic.

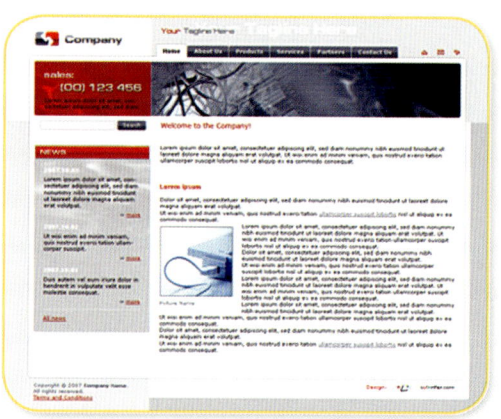

Online News channels provide easy access of latest news to those working on computers for long hours.

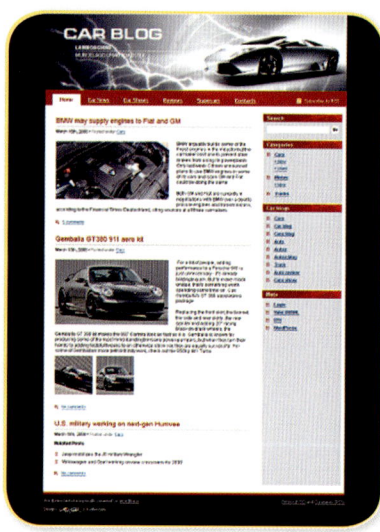

"Blog" can also be used as a verb, meaning to maintain or add content to a blog.

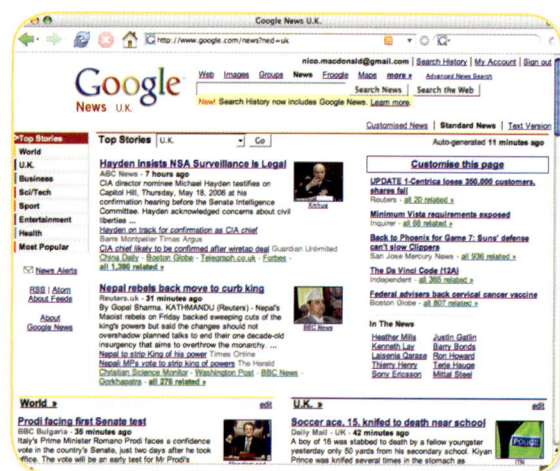

News on Google is continuously updated from thousands of sources around the world.

Google News

Google News is one of the most popular Google applications. Google News sources news from more than 4,500 news sources around the world. Google news also has a 'News Archives' section that stores old news and can automatically create timelines for events and people.

ONLINE NEWS AND BLOGS

Weblog

The term "weblog" was coined by Jorn Barger on 17th December 1997. The term 'blog' originates from "Weblog." The short form, "blog," was coined by Peter Merholz, who jokingly broke the word weblog into the phrase 'we blog' in 1999.

Blog Carnival

Blog carnival is a blog article that contains links to other articles covering a specific topic. Blog carnivals serve to generate new posts by contributors and highlight new bloggers who post matter in that subject area.

Vlog

Vlog is a video blog. A video blogger is known as a 'vlogger'. An exemple of a vlog is when someone posts a recorded version of himself while interviewing a person from a certain field.

Warblog

Warblog is a blog devoted mostly to covering news events concerning an ongoing war.

Moblog

Moblog is a term created by combining the words "mobile" and "blog". Moblog is a blog that features posts sent mainly by mobile phone, using SMS or MMS messages.

Quick Look

A book that consists of content from blogs is known as a blook.

Jorn Barger

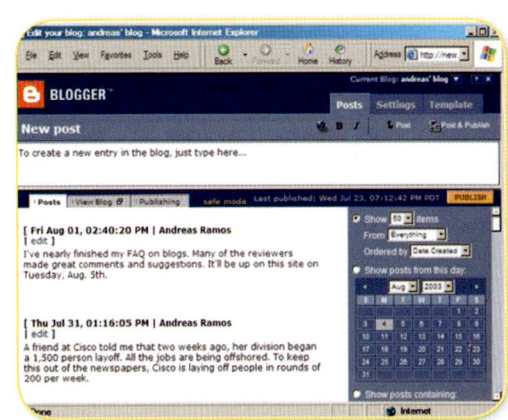

All blogs including the blogging community collectively is called Blogsphere.

Most moblogs are photoblogs.

COMMUNICATION

What is communication satellite?

A communication satellite is an artificial satellite. Communication satellites are located in space. They are used for telecommunications through signals transmitted from ground stations located on earth. Earlier, communication satellites traveled in a fixed orbit around the earth but modern ones can change their orbits.

Arthur C. Clarke

Arthur C. Clarke was an inventor and author of science fiction. He was the one who proposed satellite communication system in 1945. According to Arthur's satellite communication system, radio microwaves between distant locations on earth can be used for communication.

Arthur C. Clarke

Telstar and Syncom

Telstar was the first active satellite with a microwave receiver and transmitter. It was launched on July 10, 1962. Syncom 1 was the first synchronous satellite launched on February 13, 1963.

After the failure of Syncom 1, Syncom 2 was launched on July 26, 1963. It was more successful.

GOES-8, a United States weather satellite.

Uses of Satellite

- Microwave radio relay technology
- Mobile applications such as communications to ships, vehicles, planes and hand-held terminals
- TV and radio broadcasting, for which application of other technologies, such as cable, is impractical or impossible
- Voice communication

Satellite Communication

Earth Stations

Earth stations are transmitting and receiving stations located on distant places on earth. Earth stations are meant to send and receive communication signals. They can range from expensive to simple and cheap stations. Expensive stations can send all types of communication signals whereas cheap stations can only receive television signals. It depends on the power built into the satellite and the frequencies used.

Advantages of Communication Satellites

- Cost of communication satellite transmission is independent of area or distance
- Communication links can be extended to unreachable remote areas
- Less costly for long distance communication

Earth stations also communicate with space probes and manned spacecrafts.

Quick Look

DBS or Direct Broadcast Satellite is a communication satellite that transmits to small DBS satellite dishes (usually 5 to 7 meters in diameter).

First Communication Satellites

Satellite	First	Year
Herman Potocnik	Describes a space station in geosynchronous orbit.	1928
Arthur C. Clarke	Proposes a station in geosynchronous orbit to relay communications and broadcast television.	1945
Sputnik 1	First satellite equipped by radio-transmitters.	1957
Project SCORE	America's first communications satellite.	1958
Telstar	First satellite designed to transmit television and high-speed data communications.	1962
Syncom	First communication satellite in geosynchronous orbit.	1963
Orbita	First national TV network based on satellite television.	1967
Ekran	First serial Direct-To-Home TV communication satellite.	1976
Palapa	A1 first Indonesia communications satellite.	1976
Cassini	Spacecraft relays to Earth images from the Huygens probe as it lands on Saturn's moon, Titan, the longest relay to date.	2005

COMMUNICATION

Index

A
Academy Awards 21
alphanumeric 6
Antwerp 9
Atlantic Ocean 12
Australia 6, 9, 14-15, 23

B
BBC 13, 28
Belgium 7
Bermuda 14
Bible 5, 11
Blogsphere 29
blook 29
Braille 3
Brazil 14

C
California 6
Cambridge 11
Canada 14, 17
China 4-5, 9, 15, 27
Chinese 3-4
choir 22
Connecticut 12, 17

D
Denmark 14
Direct Broadcast Satellite 31
Dylan, Bob 18

E
Egypt 4
electronic 10, 14, 24, 26
England 22
Europe 5

F
Finland 17
Fox News 28
France 7, 14-15, 17

G
Georgia 3
German 4, 19
Germany 5, 9, 15
Greeks 4

H
Haiti 3
Han Dynasty 4
highways 24
Hollywood 20-21

I
India 9, 15
Ireland 14
Italy 7, 15

J
Japan 9, 14-15
jingles 24-25

K
Kenya 11
kinetoscope 21

L
Latvia 14
London 8, 11, 23, 25

M
Madonna 18
Massachusetts 11
Merholz, Peter 29
microwaves 30
Missouri 6

N
Netherlands 14
Network News Transport Protocol 28
New Haven 12, 17
New York 8-9, 17, 22-23
Nobel Prize 12
North America 6
Norway 14, 17
Norwich 6

O
optical fibers 17
orchestra 22
Oscars 20-21

P
Paris 7, 17
Philadelphia 17
Pfister, Albrecht 5
piano 19
Presley, Elvis 18
Proscenium 23
publicity 20, 24

R
Romania 14
Romans 4
Rowling, J. K. 10
Russia 15, 21

S
San Francisco 6
South Carolina 3
Spanish 3
Stanford University 26
Sumerian 3
Sweden 9, 17
synchronous 30

T
Tomlinson, Ray 26

U
UK 6, 11, 13-14, 23
Ukraine 15
University of Texas 19
USSR 14

V
Venice 9
violin 19

W
Washington 11
Webcam 26
World Wide Web 25, 28

X
xylography 5

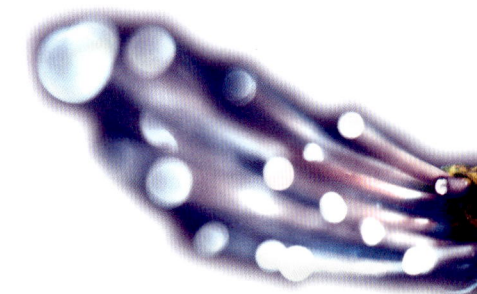

32